Medieval Places

Sarah Howarth

SIMON & SCHUSTER

LONDON • SYDNEY • NEW YORK • TOKYO • SINGAPORE • TORONTO

For Philip

First published in Great Britain in 1991 by

Simon & Schuster Young Books
Wolsey House
Wolsey Road
Hemel Hempstead
Hertfordshire HP2 4SS

Designed by Neil Adams
Illustrations by Philip McNeill

Text copyright © 1991 by Sarah Howarth
Illustrations copyright © 1991 by Philip McNeill

Typeset by DP Press Ltd, Sevenoaks

Printed and bound by Proost International Book Co, Belgium

British Library Cataloguing in Publication Data

Howarth, Sarah
  Medieval places.
  I. Title
  941.02

  ISBN 0750008784

Picture Acknowledgements

Front cover: Osterreichishe Nationalbibliothek
Spine: By courtesy of the Trustees of the British Library

Lesley & Roy Adkins Picture Library: p.39; Bibliotheque Nationale, Paris: p.16, p.19, p.33, p.35, p.44; Bibliotheque Royale, Brussels: p.10; Bodleian Library, Oxford: p.6 and p.34 MS BOD. 264 f 218v; p.27 MS BOD. 264 f 82v; By courtesy of the Trustees of the British Library: p.5, p.8; p.9, p.11, p.12, p.14, p.20, p.21, p.28, p.29, p.31, p.32, p.38, p.41, p.45; E.T. Archive: p.17, p.22, p.40; Reproduced by permission of the Provost and Fellows of Eton College: p.25, p.37; Giraudon: p.7, p.30, p.42; Sonia Halliday Photographs: p.23; Michael Holford Photographs: p.15, p.43; The Mansell Collection: p.36; By permission of the Warden and Fellows of New College, Oxford: p.3, p.26; Royal Commission on Ancient and Historical Monuments in Wales: p.13; By courtesy of the Trustees of Sir John Soane's Museum: p.18; By permission of the Masters and Fellows, Trinity College, Cambridge: p.24.

Picture research by Jennie Karrach

CONTENTS

INTRODUCTION

In this book you will learn about different medieval places and what happened in them. It will tell you how and where medieval people spent their time, about their houses, and the places in which they worked. If you want to know where people were educated, where they

went to church, where they went for justice when there was a quarrel, you can use this book to give you some of the answers. It will also tell you about where and how people enjoyed themselves, where they went to war — and how they got there.

Looking at these medieval places will help you understand a very long period of history, stretching from the fall of the Roman Empire in the fifth century AD, to the period known as the 'Renaissance' in the late fifteenth century. Society was slow to change during this time. With this book you can begin to trace some of the changes in the way people lived and the way they thought about the world. This will help you to see how the past gradually developed into the society that we live in today.

THE FIELD

This is a description of a medieval village, its fields and inhabitants:

'There is land for fifteen ploughs. There are seventeen villagers, ten smallholders, and ten slaves. There is a mill and a fishery. There are 130 acres of meadowland and an area of woodland.'

The description comes from the *Domesday Book*, the great survey of England compiled by William the Conquerer's officials in 1086. This passage tells us about a village called Faringdon, but the way of life it describes was common throughout Europe.

Life on the land

There were few towns in the Middle Ages. Most people lived in country villages, and spent their time working the land.

Year in, year out, life on the land was much the same. The farming year began in autumn. This was the time to

This medieval tapestry shows members of the nobility watching as grapes are harvested. Compare their costume with that of the peasants. What differences do you notice?

THE FIELD

Here you can see men and women at work in the fields. They are harvesting the corn, cutting it with sickles, and tying it into sheaves.

take the ploughs out into the fields and sow seed so that there would be corn the following summer. All the villagers worked together, but ploughing and sowing took weeks to complete. The ploughs were pulled by a team of oxen, and the seed was sown by hand.

Before Christmas the villagers had to collect wood for fuel, mend their tools and clear the ditches. Because there was never enough food for the village livestock over the winter, many of the animals had to be slaughtered. The meat was then salted, because this was the only way to preserve it over the months to come.

The villagers had to watch their own supplies carefully, rationing them so that there would be enough to last. As winter dragged on, supplies dwindled. The villagers longed for spring, and fresh food.

In the spring there were more crops to sow: oats, peas, beans, barley. Once the grass began to grow again, sheep and cows could be put out to graze. The cowherd went into the fields to look after the cattle, and the shepherds to look after the sheep.

Midsummer meant it was time for hay-making and sheep-shearing. In August the crops were ready to be harvested. The corn was cut with sickles (long curved knives), tied into sheaves and carted away to be stored. And then it was time to begin the cycle all over again.

The landscape

The medieval landscape looked very different from the countryside today. Two or three vast fields surrounded the village. The villagers all had a share of the land in these fields. But they could not fence their plots off. This was because their land was mixed in with their neighbours' lands — a tiny bit here and another bit there.

Historians call these great fields 'open fields'.

Each great field was used in turn. Part of the village land would always be left 'to lie fallow', that is it would not be planted with crops. It would be given extra manure, and left for the soil to improve for a year before being planted again.

These peasants are ploughing with a team of oxen. Many peasants had to farm their lord's lands as well as their own.

Manors

The villagers who worked in the fields did not usually own the land they farmed. The lord of the land allowed them to use it, in return for paying rent and working on his land. Many lords had very large estates, spread across the whole country. It was more convenient for these great men to divide their land up and run it as small units. These units were called 'manors'. Some manors were divided into two parts: the 'demesne', which was the land run directly by the lord, and the fields used by the peasants.

Working for the lord of the manor

The lord of the manor needed the villagers to work on the demesne. They produced food for his household. Any extra was sold for cash. Customs varied from place to place. Some peasants had to work almost every day for their lord. Others only had to help at the busiest times of the year.

Here a medieval lawyer lists the sort of services peasants had to perform:

'They must wash and shear the lord's sheep for three days each summer. They must weed the lord's corn for three days, and carry the hay for him. Four times a year they must cart his corn to market. They must give him 40 eggs from their hens at Easter.'

THE PEASANT'S COTTAGE

A man who lived in Italy in the thirteenth century tells a story which gives us an idea of what a peasant's cottage was like. Unhappy with conditions in one area,

'the men carried away their houses and built them elsewhere.

This picture tells us a lot about peasant life. Peasants had to spend much of their time working in the fields. They lived in small huts, like the one shown here. It has no windows and no chimney.

How cottages were made

This line tells us that peasants' houses were not great stone buildings. Most were made of timber. First a wooden framework was built. Then the spaces were filled with wattle (a network of twigs) and daub (a mixture of clay, straw and anything else that came to hand). The very poorest peasants had little more than a circular mud hut. The roof was thatched with straw or reeds, or covered with turf. Such houses were not very secure. Thieves could break in by digging through a wall, or making a hole in the roof.

To find out what the cottages were like, we have to piece information together. Archaeology, aerial photography and writing by contemporaries all help.

Archaeological excavations suggest that the smallest cottages were only fifteen feet long, and six feet wide. These belonged to the poorest

villagers, who owned no land of their own. Photographs taken from the air can show up sites which would not be easily recognized on the ground, revealing where medieval cottages have once been.

Huts like these housed both people and animals. They were built with timber frames and roughly plastered walls. The roofs were thatched.

The peasant's life

These sources tell us some of the facts and figures. The people of the time can tell us what it was actually like to live in one of these cottages. The fourteenth-century poet, Chaucer, describes the home of a poor widow and her way of life.

She lived with her daughters, three people crammed into two small rooms. Like many country people, they shared their home with their livestock — three cows and a sheep. Sometimes the animals were kept in a byre (barn) partitioned off from the living accommodation. But it was not at all unusual for chickens to wander in and out, scratching at the earthen floor, or for a cow or pig to sleep inches away from the family.

This house had two rooms, but many peasants had only one. Here the whole family ate and slept, parents, children, sometimes grandparents, all squashed together. Privacy was a luxury for the rich. The cottage would be very dark. Holes high in the walls served as windows, but they had no glass. Wind or rain blew through unless wooden shutters were put up. A fire in the middle of the floor was used for cooking. It provided some warmth, but also covered everything in soot. There was no chimney. The cottage had no running water or toilet. Water came from the nearest stream or well. It had to be carried home.

The peasant had few possessions. A trestle table, a bench, a few cooking-pots and tools, a wooden chest for clothes or food — these were all the furnishings the cottage had. Not everyone had a bed. Many had to make do with a straw mattress thrown down on the floor.

Poverty and protest

Life was hard in these conditions. The Church taught that the poor should not complain because Christ himself had lived in poverty. Most people felt that it was natural for life to be like this. They did not expect conditions to change.

As time went by, some peasants did protest. In some countries rebellion broke out. This happened in England in 1381, in France in 1358 and in Germany in 1524. Poverty was one grievance. Lack of freedom was another.

This scene shows the men who led a rebellion among the English peasants in 1381. It was drawn to illustrate a chronicle written at the time. Few people sympathized with the peasants' lot, and the revolt was crushed.

In the eyes of the law, men were not equal. There were many different groups in society. As you saw in the extract from the *Domesday Book*, slavery still existed. The peasants who had to work for the lord of the manor on his estates were only one step up from slaves. Contemporary sources call these peasants 'villeins'. They were not always the very poorest people in the village, but they had the least freedom over their lives. To have to perform labour services meant a man was not free. He was just as much the lord's property as the land itself.

THE CASTLE

A German poet who lived in the thirteenth century describes a typical medieval castle:

'The structure of the castle was splendid! People say that it is proof against any attack. Those inside hardly fear assault at all. All round the castle-hill ran a wall of cultivated trees — figs, pomegranates, olives, and many other kinds.'

The castle served two purposes: it was a stronghold and a home.

Building a castle

The first castles were fairly simple. Made of wood, they were designed to be erected quickly. Such castles are called 'motte and bailey castles'. This is how they were built. A mound of earth was made, either by piling up the soil, or by digging away at the sides of a hill to make it steeper. This mound was called the 'motte'. It was surrounded by a deep ditch, and crowned with a timber tower called a 'keep'. The 'bailey' lay at the base of the motte. It was an area enclosed by wooden stakes. The whole design was intended to keep enemies out, and give those inside as much security as possible. If there was no immediate prospect of attack, the soldiers in the castle (the garrison) lived in the bailey. When danger threatened, they withdrew to the motte, the most secure part of the site. Here they would be

The castle at Hastings, shown on page 15, was built in a day. This aerial photograph shows Beaumaris Castle in Anglesey, Wales. Work on the castle began at the end of the thirteenth century and lasted over 20 years. Money ran out before the castle was finished.

Castle defences were constantly improved. An attacking army, like the one shown here, might have to lay siege to a castle for many months before it was forced to surrender.

better able to hold out against the enemy.

Although the castle was the most secure type of building, it was possible for an attacking force to lay siege to it and eventually capture it. Throughout the Middle Ages castle design changed to improve defences and keep up with advances in the weapons used by attackers.

One important change was that stone began to be used instead of wood. A timber keep was vulnerable because the enemy could set fire to it. By the twelfth century stone had completely replaced timber, although it made castle building more expensive.

Castles and conquest

Castles were built all over Europe from the ninth century onwards. The times were violent. If a man had the power and the wealth to build a castle, he would be able to defend his land from attack. But castles were not only used for defence. They were also put up in newly conquered territory to show the local people that the castle-owner had power. A castle was a centre of power which dominated all the local area. The only other buildings in the area were the peasants' cottages, and perhaps a church.

One chronicler's story of war fought in Normandy in 1090 shows how castles were used:

'The king won the castle of Aumale and garrisoned it with his knights. From this base they attacked the land, harrying and burning. After this they seized more castles and garrisoned them with knights.'

The key to power was to control as many castles as possible.

This scene is from the Bayeux Tapestry. The tapestry tells the story of the Norman conquest of England in 1066. Here the Normans build a castle at Hastings in Sussex.

At home in the castle

The castle was a home as well as a stronghold. The lord of the castle lived there with his family, servants, horses, dogs and a large number of fighting men. The great hall was the focus of daily life. Here everyone ate and spent their free time. Most of the household slept here too, wrapped in their cloaks, as close to the fire as possible. The lord and his family slept together in a separate chamber, called a 'solar'. At meal times, only the lord had a chair. He and his family sat at a dais, a slightly raised platform at the head of the room. These things were signs of his importance. The rest of the household sat on long wooden benches. The tables were great boards set on trestle legs. They were put up at meal times, and dismantled afterwards to give more space. Belongings were stored in great wooden chests.

THE BATTLEFIELD

This account of an incident in the Hundred Years War was written by the chronicler Jean Froissart:

'The battle finished with a display of hand-to-hand fighting between six knights. The Prince and his men watched with interest. At length the French knights all stopped fighting and gave up their swords. They said "Sirs, we are your prisoners. You have beaten us." The English knights accepted them as prisoners but no mercy was shown to the rest of the army.'

Rules of warfare

Froissart's story shows us how war was fought in the Middle Ages. There were unwritten rules about the way war should be waged. The Church had affected some of these ideas. One was the belief that war should only be fought for a just cause. This meant that kings wanted to explain why they believed they were right before they committed their country to war. If they could also paint their enemy in a bad light, they did so.

Knights attacking the city of Antioch in Syria. Many knights went on Crusade when the Church proclaimed a holy war against the Saracens in 1095.

When King Edward I of England went to war with the King of Scots in the late thirteenth century, he accused the Scots of terrible crimes. Letters were sent to bishops all over the country to explain why Edward believed his cause was just. He ordered the bishops to have the letters read out to people in church. He also wrote to the pope, because he wanted his support.

People also believed that war should be fought according to the ideals of knighthood — the code of chivalry. Knights fought bravely, surrendering only if no prospect of victory remained. Froissart's story shows how this happened.

When a knight was captured, he was held prisoner. His captors were expected to behave chivalrously. They had to treat him well until his friends and family bought his freedom by paying a sum of money called a ransom. Very important people paid ransoms of thousands of pounds. A ransom made the person who received it wealthy. For the man who had to pay it, it could mean ruin.

This picture shows the Battle of Crecy, which was fought in 1346 between England and France. It was drawn to illustrate the chronicle written by Jean Froissart.

Weapons

The knight fought on horseback with a sword and lance. He wore armour and carried a shield as protection. The lance was a great wooden pole held under the arm at right angles to the body. The knight charged at his enemy, trying to topple him from his horse with the force of the blow from the lance.

Foot-soldiers fought alongside the knights on the battlefield. Archers, armed with longbows, fired arrows at the enemy. In the fourteenth century the skill of the English archers made them widely feared.

Besieging the enemy

War was a way of winning power and riches, and was often brutal. Knights did not always live up to the high ideals of chivalry. Victory depended on gaining control of key points like towns and castles. Well-defended,

Can you count the different ways in which the soldiers are attacking this walled town? Some are firing long-bows, one a cross-bow, another a cannon. Others are trying to fill in the moat so they can scale the town walls.

with high stone walls, these were not easy to capture. The attacking army might have to lay siege to them for many months. They camped outside the walls, trying to break down the defences. At the same time they stopped food supplies from being taken inside, hoping to starve the enemy into surrender.

Froissart's chronicle describes a siege:

'The army laid siege to the castle, setting up great engines to hurl missiles day and night at the towers. They did much damage. Peasants from the surrounding area were ordered to come and fill up the moat with earth and straw so that a wheeled tower could be brought right up to the walls. Then they would be able to batter at the walls.'

There would be little mercy for those inside when the castle was taken. The victors would ransack it, taking whatever they found. Jewels, fine clothes, gold plate, and furniture were all taken as booty, the profits of war.

THE FOREST

H ere a medieval Englishman describes the great
passion of the time – hunting:

*'The forest is a safe abode for wild animals, the
sanctuary and special delight of kings. There they go to
refresh themselves with a little hunting.'*

Hunting in the forest

Hunting was the most popular of medieval sports. Men
hunted for excitement and for food. All sorts of people
were enthusiastic hunters. For knights and noblemen
hunting provided practice riding and handling weapons.
These were skills useful for war. But even great ladies

*Hunting was enjoyed by
many medieval people.
Here men ride after a
deer with hunting dogs.*

went out hunting, and so did men of the Church. The poet Chaucer tells the tale of a monk who kept greyhounds and was happier hunting than praying. The clergy were often criticized for hunting instead of devoting their time to God.

The sport of kings

Hunting was above all the sport of kings and noblemen.

The German Emperor Frederick II wrote a book about hunting with falcons. Only noblemen hunted with birds of prey like the hawk or falcon. The emperor's book describes in detail how these birds were trained.

Hawks and falcons were very valuable. Training them took a long time. First they were taught to sit on the gloved wrist of their owner, then to fly at other birds and kill them before returning to their owner. In this way they were used to hunt birds like duck and partridge. The man who trained and cared for the birds was called a falconer.

Members of the nobility had particular favourites among the birds. They took the birds in to the great hall of their castle at meal times, and even let them perch by the bed at night. A medieval French writer tells a story which shows how highly prized the birds were. He writes of a knight who fights in single combat for the prize of a fine sparrowhawk. After a great fight, he wins, and presents it to his lady. The writer describes how she always keeps it at her side. When the household sits down to eat in the great hall, she 'feeds the hawk on her wrist with a plover's wing.'

The law of the forest

Other medieval rulers were as passionate huntsmen as Frederick II. In England the Norman kings turned great areas of the countryside into game parks. Only the king was allowed to hunt in them. The parks were known as forests, although they were not necessarily areas of woodland. In their enthusiasm for hunting, kings like William the Conqueror decided that land where crops

Medieval people hunted all sorts of birds and animals. Powerful birds of prey were specially trained to fly and take ducks and small birds. This picture shows a falconer, the man who cared for hawks and falcons.

were grown, and even towns and villages, would be 'forest'.

A special system of law protected the king's hunting rights in the forest. This was forest law and it allowed only the king to hunt the animals there. Occasionally he would allow a favoured subject to hunt roe deer, hares, badgers or wild cat. But the animals considered the best sport — wild boar, red and fallow deer — were kept for the king alone.

Poachers and outlaws

Under forest law, poaching was the greatest crime of all. If poachers were caught, they paid with their lives. It was a crime even to enter the forest carying a bow and arrow, let alone to use them. Poaching was a risky way of taking food, but many people took the risk. Some put themselves permanently outside the law, living in the forest on what they could hunt, and often on what they could steal from passing travellers.

The stories of Robin Hood describe this way of life. Historians do not have enough evidence to say if there really was an outlaw called Robin Hood. But they do know that the stories are very close to life. In fourteenth-century England there were bands of outlaws who took to the forest, defying the king's men and hunting his deer. Tales of Robin Hood were already being told in the Middle Ages. They were very popular. They made it plain how people hated the king's total control of hunting rights in the forest.

Rabbits were hunted for food and for sport. For the poor, it was a dangerous sport. If caught, they were punished severely.

THE LAW-COURT

In this extract a medieval Icelander describes the meeting of the *Althing*, the country's chief law-court:

'The Althing *was well attended. Most of the chieftains in the land were there. Sam the lawyer went to every one of them for their help and support against Hrafnkel, for Hrafnkel had killed a man. But each man gave the same answer: Hrafnkel was too powerful and they did not want to quarrel with him.'*

Many courts

There were many different sorts of law-court in the Middle Ages. The king's courts tried the most important cases. His barons also held courts for the people who lived on their estates. Each manor had its own court. If the villagers living on the lands of the manor did wrong, they would have to appear in this court. The Church had its own courts, where members of the clergy were tried. There were also special law-courts in the towns. These dealt with crimes committed there.

The right to hold a court was a great privilege. It was more than just a mark of importance. It was a source of profit. If people were declared guilty and fined, the man who held the court would keep the money.

In this picture of a law court, you can see the judges (sitting at the back) and the prisoners (chained up at the front). In the centre, clerks are making a record of the cases on long rolls of parchment. Historians today use these rolls to find out about crime in medieval society.

Crime and punishment

Legal records of the time can tell us about the crimes medieval people committed and how they were punished. Here are some typical cases:

'William son of Henry stole a black mare, price 16d [6½p], from the Prior of Cartmel. Richard, son of the baker, broke into a house and took 7s [35p] in pennies, stole some wool, and linen cloth. Thomas of Hellbeck

Cases took a long time to come to court. Some prisoners waited for years in squalid conditions in the dungeons of the local castle. This medieval glass depicts a wealthy man coming to visit prisoners and help them.

has taken a plot of land from William Legard. William of Dacre has unjustly taken land from William Engleys. Hugh has built a pond which takes all the water away from the watermill.'

Wrong-doers were often fined. But if the judges decided that the person accused was innocent, they would fine the one who had brought the case to court instead. Offenders were not sent to prison. People had to wait a long time for their case to come to court — sometimes years. This was when they were locked away, in the dungeon of a castle. After this the punishment was still to come.

Some punishments were intended to shame the culprit. Tradespeople who tried to cheat their customers by selling shoddy goods were punished in a variety of ways. A baker who had sold loaves which weighed less than they should have done would be dragged through the streets on a sledge, one of the bad loaves hung about his neck. Everyone would jeer. Being put in the stocks was another way of making the offender feel thoroughly foolish. It was uncomfortable too: bystanders would throw stones or any rotting vegetables which happened to be lying in the street.

Other punishments were very severe. Thieves were hanged, even if the value of the stolen goods was very low. Offenders were sometimes mutilated, having an ear or a hand cut off. This was the punishment King Henry I of England ordered in 1124 when he found that his moneyers, the men who minted coins, had been cheating him.

This picture was drawn in the middle of the twelfth century. It tells us how prisoners were punished in the Middle Ages. The man on the right is sitting in the stocks. The other two prisoners are tied up. Criminals were punished very harshly at this time.

Above the law

Although there were many different sorts of court to punish criminals, there were many people who broke the law. The tale of Hrafnkel and Sam the lawyer has already given you a glimpse of this. In every country there were men like Hrafnkel with so many followers that they could do virtually what they liked. No matter how serious the crime they committed, the victims were afraid to accuse them in court.

Because of the way some people could escape justice, medieval society was often violent and lawless. A knight who lived in the fifteenth century summed it up like this: 'Guard your gates both night and day, for thieves go about boldly like lords.'

THE SCHOOL

A twelfth-century chronicler wrote this about going to school:

'When I was five years old, I went to school. My lessons were dedicated to God. The priest taught me my letters, psalms and hymns.'

The writer was describing his own education, but many children were taught in this way. Medieval schools were very different from schools today.

Schools dedicated to God

Most medieval schools were run by the Church. They were originally founded to train men to become members of the clergy. Monks and priests had to be able to read and write so they could take part in religious services. They were among the very few people who received an education in the Middle Ages.

There were schools in important monasteries and cathedrals, and sometimes in smaller churches. These schools concentrated on teaching subjects useful for the Church. At about the age of seven, a boy could enter the 'song' school of a Cathedral school. Here he would learn the Latin chants and responses for the services.

The poet Chaucer describes what boys learned in schools like this. He explains how they learned to read from books of prayers, and to sing special prayers like the *Ave Maria*, a Latin prayer of devotion to the Virgin Mary. This shows the importance of religion in all the teaching at these schools. Chaucer's story also shows us another central fact about medieval education: the importance of Latin.

Since the days when the Romans ruled much of the known world, their language, Latin, had been used by writers and scholars in many countries. It was an almost

A school-master with his pupils. Few children received an education in the Middle Ages. For centuries learning was restricted to boys who were going to enter the Church.

Wealthy men and women often gave money to schools and churches in the Middle Ages. This scene shows William of Wykeham, one of the most important ministers of King Edward III of England, and the school he founded at Winchester. The school still survives today.

universal language. Authors wrote in Latin rather than the vernacular (the language of their own country) for many hundreds of years. Latin was also used by the Church. The Bible, church services and prayers were all in Latin. For these reasons, much school time was spent on Latin. After the song school, boys could enter a 'grammar' school. Here they learned more about the Latin language, concentrating on the rules of grammar. These explain how the language should be written.

In class

Teachers were expected to be hard on their pupils. Beatings were frequent. This medieval poem shows that severe punishments were common in the schools of the time:

'Clever teacher, is it your
Intent to beat us more and more
Like a blooming lord?'

There were few books in the schools. They were rare and expensive, and only the teacher would have one. He read aloud to the pupils, who had to learn all their lessons by heart. Any writing was done on pieces of slate, or wax tablets, which could be used over and over again. This was because of the cost of writing materials like paper and parchment.

Different sorts of education

It was not compulsory for children to go to school in the Middle Ages. The children of peasant families were lucky if they had any education. For most of them, there was no schooling, just hard work. They had to help their parents work in the fields as soon as they were able.

The children of townsfolk were usually trained for a career in trade. Merchants had to be able to read, write and keep accounts for their business. Some towns set up schools to teach such skills. They were among the few schools not run by the Church.

The children of knights and barons were brought up to lead lives like those of their parents. Aged ten, or even younger, they were sent away from home to be brought up in another household. This was meant to make them grow up quickly. It was also a way for important families to maintain good relations with each other. The sons of knights learned all the skills they would need to become knights themselves. They were trained to ride and handle weapons. Girls learned the tasks performed by the lady of the castle. They had to sew, make clothes, cook, prepare medicines and manage servants.

This picture shows a boy learning some of the skills he would need to become a knight. He is practising riding with a lance at a special target called a quintain.

THE UNIVERSITY

A famous twelfth-century teacher named Peter Abelard tells us this story, describing how he started a school almost by chance:

'I took myself off to a lonely place in France. With the permission of the bishop of that area, I built a small chapel out of reeds and thatch. Here I meant to live by myself. But as soon as people heard that I lived in this place, students began to arrive there, hurrying from towns and cities to learn from me.'

The discipline in medieval schools was severe. This picture shows scholars being beaten on their hands with a 'palmer'.

Wandering scholars

This is the way great schools and universities developed. Teachers like Abelard, who were respected for their learning, found that wherever they went, people would follow them, keen to listen to what they had to say. The students who travelled from place to place in search of teachers were called wandering scholars. There were many of these scholars in the eleventh and twelfth centuries. Many were young men, some only just out of their teens, while others were much older. There was no age limit. It was a very informal way of gaining an education.

The scholars covered great distances to learn from thinkers whose reputation had reached them. One scholar, a man named Gerbert, who came from Rheims in France, visited Italy, Germany and Spain in his quest for knowledge. This was typical of the way of life of the wandering scholars.

The teachers who attracted the wandering scholars were to be found in many places. Some taught in monastery or cathedral schools. There were important schools of this sort in France and Italy. Other teachers, like Abelard, set up schools of their own. They had to have the Church's permission to do this because the Church controlled nearly every aspect of education. The success of all these schools depended on the quality of the teachers. Scholars flocked to hear those who lectured well. But if the students were disappointed by what and how they were taught, they would leave and go somewhere else.

Until the fifteenth century, all books and documents were hand-written, not printed. Scribes, working like the one here, made copies of the original manuscript. The word manuscript means 'something written by hand'.

The beginnings of a settled way of life

Today universities are highly organized institutions. They are based in particular towns and operate from permanent buildings. They offer set courses in many subjects. Abelard's story of the wandering scholars shows us that their education was not organized in this way. The great schools of his time grew up on the reputation of individual teachers. They were set up with very little planning and could disappear just as rapidly. But it was out of these schools that the university system we have today developed.

The word 'university' comes from the Latin language. It was first used in the thirteenth century. At this time it simply meant a group of people, a club rather like a trade guild. People used the word to describe a group of students or a group of teachers. Little by little, these 'universities' of students and teachers became more settled. The life of the wandering scholars became a thing of the past. Rules were made to govern the students' way of life. Courses of study were organized. Colleges were built to house the students. Examinations were set.

Peter Abelard and his wife, Heloise. This couple lived in France in the twelfth century. Abelard won fame as a scholar and teacher. He taught at the University of Paris. Heloise became a nun. She was widely respected for her learning.

Many universities were established in the Middle Ages. One of the oldest was the Moslem university of the Karaouine at Fez in Morocco, which was established in the ninth century. By the fourteenth century many European countries also had universities. In Bohemia (today called Czechoslovakia), King Charles IV established the university of Prague in 1348. The universities of Paris, Oxford and Salerno (in Italy) were among the first in Europe.

The students' life

Studying at university took many years. There was no fixed age to begin. Some boys started their university education at the age of thirteen. For the first seven years, they all studied the same subjects. These were Latin grammar, rhetoric (the art of speaking), logic (the art of composing reasoned arguments), arithmetic, geometry, music and astronomy. After this period they were free to specialize in law, medicine, or theology (the study of God). They learned by attending lectures and special debates called 'disputations'. Many students were very poor, too poor even to buy books.

THE ROAD

This is the chronicler Froissart describing an occasion of great splendour – the queen's arrival in Paris:

'On Sunday 20 August 1389, there were great crowds of people in Paris and its outskirts. They had come to see the young Queen enter the city. Twelve hundred citizens of Paris were drawn up on horseback on either side of the road. The Queen and her ladies travelled in covered litters with a large escort of noblemen. The litters were richly decorated. The horses drawing them went at walking pace.'

The details that Froissart includes tell us much about medieval travel.

Travel in the Middle Ages

Travel in the Middle Ages was slow and uncomfortable. There were two choices open to medieval travellers. They could go on foot, or on horseback if they could afford to do so. Wealthy and important ladies travelled in horse-drawn litters like those in Froissart's story. This was the height of luxury in medieval travel. But the state of the roads was so bad that even this form of transport was uninviting.

Nobles spent much time travelling between the different parts of their estates. The men rode on horseback, whilst the women travelled in richly decorated carriages like this. The drawing comes from an English manuscript called the Luttrell Psalter.

This picture shows a cross being put up at a cross-roads. There were many crosses and chapels by the roadside so the traveller could pray for a safe journey.

The Romans had built a great network of roads, which were still in use in the Middle Ages, although now they were in a poor state of repair. Little maintenance work was done on them, so they became full of ruts and pot-holes. Despite their bad condition, these were the main roads of the time. Other roads were little more than muddy tracks across the countryside. Travellers had no choice but to go slowly. Their horses stumbled in the cracks in the road surface, and sank in boggy ground. In winter it was often impossible to travel by road. Floods and bad weather could close them completely. In these conditions, even the shortest journey could be difficult.

Robbers on the roads and byways

The state of the roads was not the only danger facing the medieval traveller. Listen to what these medieval people had to say about journeys they had undertaken. What was their greatest worry?

'*Whenever my enemies heard that I was about to set out on a journey, they would bribe robbers and station them on the roads and byways to murder me.*'

This was written by a Frenchman in the twelfth century. His fear of robbers was not unusual. Travellers were frequently attacked by thieves.

'Merchants dared not ride about to do their business for fear of being robbed. Their money was snatched away, leaving them with nothing.'

Here a chronicler describes the fear of English travellers at the end of the fourteenth century. The problem was not confined to England. All over Europe, travellers went in fear. They preferred to travel in groups for safety.

The travellers

Despite the dangers, there were many travellers on the roads in the Middle Ages. There were peasants carrying produce from the fields to market, or carting goods for the lord of the manor. There were knights and noblemen, riding from one part of their estates to another. As they owned lands scattered all over the country, they spent much time travelling. There were judges and criminals on their way to court; soldiers going to join the army; messengers carrying letters; merchants journeying in search of trade.

Here you can see groups of dancers and performers. They too spent a great deal of time on the road, journeying to castles and important houses to entertain the inhabitants.

All these travellers were going about their daily work. Some others had different reasons for travelling. Groups of pilgrims thronged the roads of medieval Europe on their way to pray at distant shrines. The fourteenth-century poet Chaucer tells us that pilgrims came from many walks of life: they could be knights, ploughmen, monks, nuns, cooks, sailors, lawyers, doctors, millers.

All sorts of people went on pilgrimage. Scholars took to the road on their way to great schools and universities. There were huntsmen chasing game. Troupes of wandering entertainers — acrobats, musicians and poets — were also to be seen on the road.

THE PORT

A medieval writer describes a sea journey across the Mediterranean and arrival at port in the Middle East in these words:

'When we reached port, the keepers of the port ran to our ship at once. They came on board and wrote down the names of all on the ship. They looked very carefully through all the goods we had on board and made a list of them.'

Travellers and traders

The port was a busy place. Because it was cheaper for merchants to carry their goods by sea than over land, there were always ships coming and going. The port was full of noise and activity. Newcomers talked

Here a painter has drawn the busy port of Venice. Some merchants wait on the quay for ships to arrive with new cargoes, whilst others sell their goods. Italian ports like Venice and Genoa thrived on sea-borne trade between the East and the West.

excitedly in foreign languages. Sea-captains shouted orders to their sailors. Merchants boasted about their wares.

There were all sorts of people to be seen crowding into the port. Pilgrims who had come to pray at the shrine of a local saint disembarked. Scholars travelling to study at a foreign university arrived. There were royal messengers arriving on important diplomatic missions. There were men of the Church too. Some travelled on the pope's business, sent with important letters. Some were on their way to meet the pope, to ask his advice. Even monks, who had vowed to shut themselves away from society, sometimes had to travel overseas. They were to be seen at the port on their way to the great monastic councils held to discuss matters affecting monasteries all over Europe.

'Merchandise comes from every land'

A twelfth-century writer describes how ships arrive in port with goods to sell: *'Merchandise comes from every land where Christian merchants go.'* In fact, as the account of the journey to the Middle East shows us, medieval merchants traded with men of many different lands, not just with Christian countries. Trade with the Saracens, as the Moslem inhabitants of the Middle East were called, was particularly profitable.

It was the merchants of Italy who prospered the most from this trade. As their country was placed halfway between the eastern and western trading nations, they were in a good geographical position to dominate the trade. Italian cities on the coast, like Genoa and Venice,

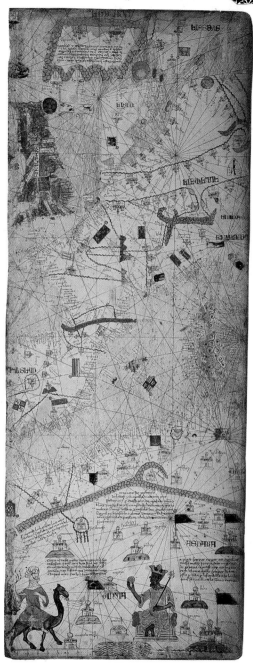

There were many parts of the world which the people of medieval Europe knew nothing about. Their maps look strange to us because of this.

became very wealthy as a result. Their ships sailed to Egypt and the East to buy sugar, cotton and spices like cinnamon, pepper, saffron and cloves. They then carried this cargo to other countries for sale. In the fourteenth century, for example, a Venetian fleet sailed regularly with these goods to Flanders, England and northern Europe. Once the goods were sold, it was time to return. But the merchants never sailed home empty-handed. During their trip away, they bought a supply of English wool, woollen cloth, tin, lead, cheese and leather. The ships were loaded once more and this time there was a cargo for sale at home.

This picture shows medieval ship-builders at work. It was drawn by a German in the fifteenth century. Medieval ships were powered by sails and oars.

New worlds

The people of medieval Europe had only a limited knowledge of the earth's geography. Traders and travellers had made their way to India. Some had explored parts of Africa. These places appear on contemporary maps. But there was still much that was not known about such distant countries.

At the end of the thirteenth century, Marco Polo, who came from Venice, wrote a description of his travels in another little-known land, China. The information brought back by travellers like Marco Polo made people realize that there were new worlds to explore.

It was the search for trading opportunities that prompted these voyages of exploration. This was what spurred a Genoese man called Christopher Columbus to set sail from a Spanish port in 1492. On his voyage Columbus landed in America, a continent Europeans knew nothing about. His voyage was to have far-reaching effects on the history of Europe.

THE PARISH CHURCH

A medieval French poet describes his old mother in the parish church where she worshipped each week:

'I am a poor old woman,
Knowing nothing: I cannot read
But in the parish church I see
Painted pictures of heaven
And hell, where the damned are burnt.
One makes me happy, the other frightens me.

The Christian Church was divided up into different units of land, and the parish was one of these. It was the smallest unit. Many parishes were about the size of a village, but some were a little larger. Each parish had a church for the local people. It was run by the parish priest.

Many churches had pictures like this painted on their walls. They depicted the punishment of sinners in hell and the reward of good people in heaven. Here sinners are being burnt up by the fiery breath of fabulous horses.

The centre of religious life

Religion was very important to medieval people, and the parish church was the centre of their religious life. There were special religious services to mark nearly every stage of life, from the cradle to the grave. Babies were brought to the parish church to be baptized by the parish priest. Children were confirmed in their faith there by the bishop. Weddings took place there, but not inside the church: they were conducted in front of the church door. And of course funerals were conducted there too, before burial took place in the church-yard. Each week local people went to Mass in the church. They also went to church to confess their sins to the priest. This usually happened once a year. The parish priest had many responsibilities. He took all the services and taught his parishioners (the people of the parish) about Christianity. Some priests found this a difficult job because they had not had enough training.

Learning about the faith

It was in the parish church that ordinary people had the opportunity to find out about their religion. But there were problems. Because church services and the Bible were in Latin, most people could not understand what was going on. Very few people could read. To learn about their faith, they therefore had to depend on what the parish priest told them in his sermons.

The story above about the poet's mother shows us another way in which the parish church was important. The building itself was designed to teach people about Christianity. Many parish churches were splendid buildings. They had expensive stained glass windows. Pictures were painted on the walls, and much of the stonework was decorated with carvings.

These things were not simply decorations. They had a practical purpose. They were there to help people learn about the Church's teaching. The windows depicted scenes from the Bible, like the story of Adam and Eve or Noah and the Ark. There were carvings of saints and apostles, of Christ and the

The men and women of the neighbourhood went to their parish church for baptisms, weddings and for funerals – like the one shown here. The parish church was the centre of their religious life.

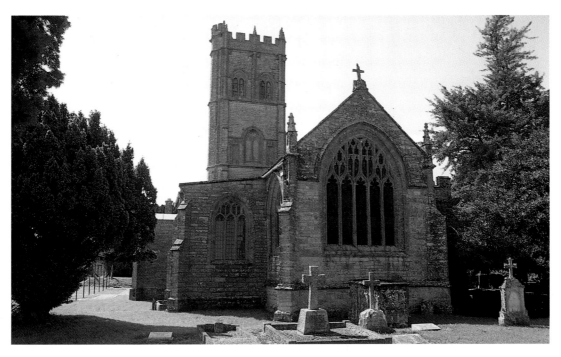

Virgin Mary. For many people, the statues and pictures in the parish church were the only form of religious teaching they would ever receive.

The heart of community life

The parish church was more than just the centre of religious life. It was used for many other purposes as well. Most were built of stone, and so were much more secure than the wooden cottages belonging to the peasants. For this reason, they were sometimes used as a safe place to store valuables. In some parishes, the church was used as a school, or as a hospital where sick people could rest. Meetings were held in the church to discuss important local issues.

The church-yard was also used by local people for a variety of pursuits. Dances and games took place here. After weddings and baptisms, special celebrations took place in the church-yard, with feasting and ale drinking. In some places markets were held in the church-yard. Bishops disapproved of such activities taking place on Church ground. But although they gave orders for these practices to stop, people took little notice.

If you compare this photograph of a medieval church with the pictures of peasants' cottages earlier in the book, you will see how the church would have towered over all the other buildings in the village. People felt that it was right for a building dedicated to God to be grand and important.

THE MARKET

This is how a group of medieval townsmen described the local market:

'A crowd of people gather to buy and sell corn, flour, beans, peas, cloth, fish and meat and other goods.'

Going to market

Markets were held in towns all over Europe. Most were held once a week, but in some places they were held more often. The townsmen were busy traders. They did not have the time to grow all their own food. On market day people from the village in the neighbourhood came to town, bringing eggs, cheese, fruit, vegetables, livestock and all sorts of other produce to sell.

Small stalls were set up in a square at the heart of town, or in one of the streets, and buyers soon crowded round to see what was on sale. It was not only the people who brought their wares to sell who made a profit on market day. So did the lord who owned the land where the market was held. Those coming to market had to pay a tax on the goods they brought with them. This was called a toll. They also had to pay to put up their stalls.

Royal permission was necessary to hold a market. The king would grant a charter stating the day on which the market was to be held, and other details. He received a sum of money in return for the charter. Many people wanted to have a market on their land.

This picture shows a butcher's stall in a meat market in Bohemia (modern Czechoslovakia). How many different sorts of meat are being sold? Is it all from animals still eaten today?

Sometimes they wanted to start a new market close to a place where one already existed. This would lead to complaints if it took trade away from the old established market. The king and his officials had to decide whether or not to allow the new market.

Shopping in town

The market added to the daily bustle and commotion of town life. The fourteenth-century English poet William Langland describes the noisy scene as sellers shout out the bargains they have to offer:

'Cooks and their boys cried "Hot pies, hot!
Good geese and pork! Come and eat!"
Inn-keepers cried the same:
"White wine from Alsace, wine from Gascony!"'

Shopping in the Middle Ages was very different from today. Shops were small and carried a limited range of goods. The stock was made by the shop-keeper himself. Here a customer looks at combs and mirrors in a perfumery shop.

The streets in town were lined with small shops. The shops belonged to craftsmen who lived and worked on the premises. They were more like work shops than shops as we know them today. It was the custom for the craftsmen to sit and work at a bench at the front of the shop. The shop was open to the street, so passers-by could inspect the standard of workmanship. There were few goods on display. Craftsmen usually worked to the customer's orders. They did not carry a large stock of finished items.

A place of contrasts

To country people who came to town, everything could seem bewildering. There was much to see, so much choice, so much money changing hands. Life in town was vastly different from the way of life they knew. In the village there were just a few one-storey cottages and perhaps a church. In town, there were two and three-storey buildings on every side. Because space in town was limited, the houses were tall and narrow, their

In this shop two wealthy men talk whilst the merchants weigh a selection of jewellery. Can you see the necklaces hanging on display?

upper storeys jutting out above the street below, and blocking out much of the light.

The streets were full of rubbish. Householders threw all their rubbish in the road. There were no drains, no indoor bathrooms or toilets. Pigs and dogs wandered about in the streets, rooting in the piles of rotting vegetables, and heaps of dung. You can imagine what it smelt like.

'To great peril of the people'

Some towns made efforts to keep the streets clean and punish the worst offenders. In medieval London, for example, action was taken against inn-keepers who left barrels blocking the street, and those who heaped rubbish outside their houses '*to great peril of the people.*' But the problem continued. The streets of most medieval towns were very dirty and evil-smelling indeed.

THE GUILD-HALL

he poet Chaucer gives us a picture of typical guild members. The guild-hall was the headquarters of such men as:

'A haberdasher and a carpenter,
A weaver, a dyer and a tapestry-maker . . .
Each of them seemed a proud townsman
Eager to sit in the guild-hall.'

This window shows men making stained glass. In the Middle Ages guild members sometimes paid for windows like this for their local church.

The guilds

Guilds were organizations run by medieval merchants and craftsmen to regulate the way business was done. They controlled the price of goods, the standard of craftsmanship and, most important of all, they decided who could do business. Guild members had a monopoly on certain trades; that means they were the only people allowed to buy and sell the goods involved in those trades.

Many different trades were involved. A list drawn up in one city in the fourteenth century shows the many sorts of business organized in this way. It tells us that there were guilds of grocers, fish-

THE GUILD-HALL

The houses of merchants and townsmen were much more comfortable than the cottages of the peasants. Here a merchant warms himself by a great fireplace and his wife spins.

mongers, drapers, goldsmiths, woolmongers, vintners (merchants who sold wine), ironmongers, cordwainers (who made and sold shoes), saddlers and butchers.

Guilds were very powerful groups, and they were important in town government. They met at the guild-hall to discuss town business and guild regulations. There was a social side to their meetings too. Great feasts were held for members. On these occasions the table in the guild-hall was loaded with sparkling gold and silver plate, and many toasts were drunk.

Guilds also tried to look after their members when they fell on hard times. Each guild member contributed to a common fund which could be used in emergencies. One guild in medieval London arranged to pay 14d (about 6p) each week to members who fell ill or became feeble when the grew old. It also had plans to help members whose trade suffered '*through fire or flood or thieves*'. Many guilds had arrangements like this.

Guild members also had religious duties. Many guilds devoted themselves to a particular saint. They had a special church service to celebrate the saint's feast day.

Masters and apprentices

Guilds supervised the training of new members very carefully. A boy who wanted to learn a trade first had to find a master craftsman prepared to take him on. He would have to agree to work for this man for a set number of years until he had learnt all the basic skills of the trade. This period was called his apprenticeship.

While he was an apprentice, the boy lived with his master's family. Conditions were often harsh. He would have to work very hard. Some apprentices were not given enough to eat. Most were beaten from time to time by the masters. They were not allowed to leave before the training was finished. Runaways were brought back by force.

When he had served his apprenticeship, the boy rose to become a 'journeyman'. This meant that he was free to work for anyone. He was paid by the day for his work. To become a master craftsman, and a full member of the guild, the journeyman had to pass a special test. He had to present a piece of work to the masters of the guild — his 'masterpiece'. If they agreed that it was good enough, he was passed as a master craftsman. Now he could train apprentices of his own.

A way to wealth

Some master craftsmen became very wealthy. They were able to build fine houses in town and buy land in the country. They and their wives could afford to dress in the latest fashions, in splendid furs and elaborate costumes. In many countries merchants were criticized, but it was not only because of their extravagance. They were criticized simply for being merchants. This was because many people believed that trade was not respectable, and that it was bad to be associated with it.

The guildhall was the meeting place for merchants and craftsmen of different guilds. Here they discussed business and also met for feasts. This illustration shows a meeting in progress. The craftsmen are carrying the tools of their trade.

Glossary

Abbot   The monk in charge of an abbey and the monks living there.

Althing   The chief law court of medieval Iceland.

Baron   An important nobleman.

Byre   A cow-house.

Charter   A document written on a piece of parchment. Charters were used to make important announcements and grant privileges.

Chivalry   A code of conduct for knights to follow. They were to protect the weak, women and the Church.

Chronicler   The person who wrote a chronicle (story of events).

Cordwainer   The person who made and sold shoes.

Daub   A mixture of mud, clay, and anything else handy. It was used in building work as a sort of plaster.

Demesne   The part of a landed estate kept under the control of the landowner, and farmed for his or her own use.

Domesday Book   A record of nearly all the land in England made by the officials of King William I. It was completed in 1086.

Estate   The lands of a wealthy person.

Falconer   The person who trained and looked after birds of prey used for hunting.

Feudal system   A word historians use to describe medieval society. In theory, every man had a lord whom he obeyed, receiving land and protection in return. For example, the peasant served the lord of the manor, and the lord of the manor served the king. In reality it was very much more complicated.

Guild   An association of merchants and craftsmen. Members discussed business and also looked after those who fell on hard times.

Habit   The special robe worn by men and women who took religious vows and entered the monastic life.

Journeyman   A craftsman who had finished his training as an apprentice, and was no longer tied to one master. Instead he could hire himself out as a workman by the day to anyone.

Knight   A warrior who fought on horseback. Knights were encouraged to be brave and loyal, and to defend the poor and weak.

Lance   A weapon used by knights. It was a long wooden shaft with which the knight tried to topple his enemy from his horse.

Longbow   A weapon used by a soldier called an archer. To fire the arrow, the string of the bow was drawn back by hand.

Manor   A country estate or farm belonging to a wealthy person.

Miller   The person who worked the mill, grinding corn to make flour for bread. Some mills were powered by water, others by wind.

Motte and bailey castle   One of the earliest sorts of castle, consisting of earthworks and a timber tower.

Pilgrim   A person who travelled to pray at the shrine of a saint.

Poacher   Someone who went hunting on another person's land.

Quintain   A target set up for weapons practice. The knight would charge his horse at the quintain, and try to strike it with his lance.

Rosary beads   A string of beads used to say special prayers and count them. A prayer to the Virgin Mary was said at each small bead, and the Lord's Prayer at each larger one.

Solar   A special room in the manor house or castle for the lord and his family. They could relax here in privacy, away from the crowded great hall.

Stocks   A wooden contraption in which people were made to sit as a punishment. The stocks fitted over the offender's ankles so he or she could not move.

Tonsure   The top of a man's head was shaved when he became a monk. This was called receiving the tonsure.

Villein   An unfree peasant. He or she had no legal rights and had to work for his or her lord in the fields.

Wattle   A mesh of twigs, plastered over with daub, used for walls and partitions in medieval homes.

Further Reading

For Children

Simon Adams, *Trade and Religion – A Historical Atlas*, Kingfisher, 1989.

Mike Corbishley, *The Middle Ages – A Cultural Atlas for Young People*, Facts On File, 1989.

Fiona Macdonald, *A Medieval Castle*, Simon & Schuster Young Books, 1991.

Fiona Macdonald, *A Medieval Cathedral*, Simon & Schuster Young Books, 1991.

R J Unstead, *Castles*, A & C Black, 1970.

For Adults

R A Brown, *English Medieval Castles*, London, 1954.

Philippe Contamine, *War in the Middle Ages*, trans. Michael Jones, Basil Blackwell, 1984.

Colin Platt, *The English Medieval Town*, Secker and Warburg, 1976.

M M Postan, *The Medieval Economy and Society*, Weidenfeld and Nicolson, 1972.